THE ORIGINAL
Country Bob's
——— COOKBOOK ———

Cooking Club of America
Member Tested & Recommended

The Original Country Bob's Cookbook
Published by Country Bob, Inc.

Copyright © 2005 by Country Bob, Inc.
P.O. Box 706 • Centralia, Illinois 62801
618-533-2375

This cookbook is a collection of favorite recipes, which are not necessarily original recipes.

The definitions of our strongly held beliefs listed on page 5 and on the chapter openers are inspired by the reading of scripture but are not direct quotations. All direct quotations of Bible verses come from the New International Version, copyright 1973, 1978, and 1984, by the International Bible Society.

Library of Congress Control Number: 2004108287
ISBN: 0-9754441-0-7

Edited, Designed, and Manufactured by Favorite Recipes® Press
An Imprint of

FRP

P.O. Box 305142
Nashville, Tennessee 37230
800-358-0560

Art Director: Steve Newman • Book Design: Brad Whitfield and Susan Breining
Photography: Cover and page 83, ©Mike Rutherford;
page 7, ©FoodPix / Steven Mark Needham;
page 33, ©FoodPix / Ross Durant; page 49, ©FoodPix / Mark Thomas.
Project Editor: Georgia Brazil • Project Manager: Ashley Bienvenu

Printed in Mexico
First Printing: 2005   10,000 copies

Introduction

How does anything really good get its start? Where do great products come from? Usually, they are the result of much time being spent and a tremendous amount of love being invested. That's the way Country Bob Edson created his All Purpose Sauce.

In 1968, Country Bob perfected the sauce of his dreams. After years of giving the sauce to friends, he began to sell it in 1977. The reaction was overwhelming. Everyone who tried it loved it! And why not, it is the perfect complement to practically any meal.

In 1982, Country Bob, Incorporated, became a reality. Bob Edson, Terry Edson, Al Malekovic, and Reed Malekovic formed a corporation and dedicated themselves to producing the best product possible with the help of their valued employees. Since then, very special family and friends have purchased stock to help make the company what it is today, with regional distribution spreading in all directions from the home base in Centralia, Illinois. But even with this tremendous growth, the men and women who are Country Bob's have never lost sight of the main focus —
the pursuit of product excellence.

It would be nice if we could claim responsibility for the success of the company; however, credit must be given where credit is due. Proverbs 16:3 says, "Commit to the Lord whatever you do, and your plans will succeed." We have placed true ownership of Country Bob, Incorporated, in the hands of God. "Christ is our CEO," and He is an awesome boss!

Table of Contents

We Believe

...in the one eternal God, Creator, Lord, and Savior of the world. God is the Father, Son, and Holy Spirit who governs all things to the purpose of His will.

(1 Corinthians 15:1-8)

...that Jesus Christ is the one and only Son of God, who died for our sins and arose from the dead.

(John 3:16)

...that the Bible is the inspired word of God — a lamp unto our feet and a light unto our path.

(2 Timothy 3:16 and Psalm 119:105)

...that every person has worth as a creation of God, but that all have sinned and fall short of the glory of God.

(Romans 3:23)

...that those accepting Christ should repent of sin, confess their faith, and be baptized into Him.

(Romans 10:9 and Acts 2:38)

...that the Church is the body of Christ on earth, empowered by the Holy Spirit and exists to bring lost people to know Jesus as Savior and Lord.

(Ephesians 4:1-16)

...that Jesus Christ will one day return to earth and reign forever as King of kings and Lord of lords.

(1 Thessalonians 4:13-18)

Appetizers, Soups, and Snacks

We Believe

...in the one eternal God, Creator, Lord, and Savior of the world. God is the Father, Son, and Holy Spirit, who governs all things to the purpose of His will.

(1 Corinthians 15:1-8)

...that Jesus Christ is the one and only Son of God, who died for our sins and arose from the dead.

(John 3:16)

Wingettes

5 pounds chicken wings
4 cups flour
$1/4$ cup granulated garlic
4 teaspoons Country Bob's Seasoning Salt
$1/4$ teaspoon red pepper
Oil for deep-frying
$1/2$ cup Country Bob's All Purpose Sauce

Cut off and discard the wing tips and separate each wing into 2 pieces at the joint if desired. Rinse the chicken wings; drain and set aside. Combine the flour, granulated garlic, Country Bob's Seasoning Salt and red pepper in a double thickness paper bag and shake until well mixed. Add the wings, several at a time, and shake until coated. Heat the oil to 350 degrees in a deep fryer. Add the wings, several at a time, to the hot oil and fry for 10 minutes or until golden brown. Drain on paper towels and place in a large bowl. Add the desired amount of Country Bob's All Purpose Sauce and toss lightly until coated. Serve with additional sauce.

Yield: variable

Country Bob's Chip Dip

1 pound lean ground beef
1 cup chopped green bell pepper
1 cup chopped onion
Salt to taste
8 ounces cream cheese
1/2 cup Country Bob's All Purpose Sauce

Cook the ground beef, green pepper and onion in a skillet until brown and crumbly, stirring frequently. Drain the ground beef mixture and return to the skillet. Season with salt. Chop the cream cheese into pieces and add to the skillet with Country Bob's All Purpose Sauce. Heat over low heat until the cream cheese melts, stirring frequently. Serve hot with favorite sturdy chips.

Yield: 4 to 5 cups

We Believe

I pray that you may be active in sharing your faith, so that you will have a full understanding of every good thing we have in Christ.

Philemon 1:6

Hot Reuben Dip

8 ounces cream cheese, softened
1 1/2 cups (6 ounces) shredded Swiss cheese
1/2 cup Thousand Island dressing
1/3 cup Country Bob's All Purpose Sauce
4 ounces deli-sliced corned beef, chopped
1/2 cup sauerkraut, drained

Combine the cream cheese, 1 cup Swiss cheese, dressing and Country Bob's All Purpose Sauce in a bowl and mix well. Stir in the corned beef. Spread the mixture in a 9-inch deep-dish pie plate or quiche pan. Top with the sauerkraut and remaining 1/2 cup Swiss cheese. Bake at 400 degrees for 15 minutes or until bubbly around the edge. Serve hot with pretzel crackers or cocktail rye bread slices.

Yield: 2 1/2 cups (about 10 servings)

We Believe
Now to him who is able to do immeasurably more than all we ask or imagine, according to his power that is at work within us, to him be glory in the church and in Christ Jesus throughout all generations, for ever and ever! Amen.

Ephesians 3:20-21

Creamy Vegetable Dip

8 ounces cream cheese, softened
$1/4$ cup Country Bob's All Purpose Sauce
$1/4$ cup (1 ounce) grated Parmesan cheese
1 teaspoon chili sauce
$1/4$ teaspoon each garlic salt and paprika
$1/2$ teaspoon celery salt

Blend the cream cheese and Country Bob's All Purpose Sauce in a bowl.
Add the remaining ingredients and mix well. Chill until serving time. Serve
with assorted bite-sized fresh vegetables for dipping.

Yield: $1 1/2$ cups

Tangy Cocktail Dipping Sauce

$1/2$ cup Country Bob's All Purpose Sauce
$1/2$ cup chili sauce
2 tablespoons lemon juice
3 tablespoons prepared horseradish

Mix all the ingredients in a small bowl. Chill for 1 hour. Use as dip for
seafood pieces, breaded vegetables, breaded chicken pieces or French fries.

Yield: 1 cup

Super Salsa

2 (15-ounce) cans black beans
1 (11-ounce) can whole kernel corn, drained
1 cup chunk-style salsa
1 medium red bell pepper, diced
3 scallions, sliced
1/2 cup chopped cilantro
1/2 cup Country Bob's All Purpose Sauce
1 tablespoon lime juice
1 teaspoon ground cumin
1/2 teaspoon garlic powder
Salt and pepper to taste

Drain the beans; rinse and drain well. Combine the beans, drained corn, salsa, red pepper, scallions and cilantro in a bowl. Add the Country Bob's All Purpose Sauce, lime juice, cumin, garlic powder, salt and pepper and mix gently. Serve immediately or store in an airtight container in the refrigerator for up to 3 days.

Yield: 6 cups

Family Reunion Cheese Balls

24 ounces cream cheese, softened
$1/2$ teaspoon minced garlic
3 tablespoons Country Bob's All Purpose Sauce
1 tablespoon hot pepper sauce
4 cups (16 ounces) shredded Cheddar cheese
1 cup chopped pecans
$1/4$ cup chopped fresh parsley

Combine the cream cheese, garlic, Country Bob's All Purpose Sauce and hot pepper sauce in a food processor or blender and process until blended. Add the Cheddar cheese and pulse until mixed but with Cheddar flakes still visible. Divide into several portions and shape into balls or logs as desired. Wrap each in plastic wrap and refrigerate or freeze. Grind the pecans and mix with the parsley on waxed paper. Just before serving, roll the cheese balls in the pecan mixture to coat. Place on serving plates and serve at room temperature with assorted crackers.

Yield: variable

Horseradish Cream Sauce

1 (4-ounce) jar prepared horseradish, drained
$1/3$ cup mayonnaise
$1/2$ cup sour cream
1 tablespoon Dijon mustard
$1/3$ cup Country Bob's All Purpose Sauce
$1/4$ teaspoon salt
2 tablespoons parsley
2 shallots, minced
$1/2$ cup whipping cream, whipped

Combine the horseradish, mayonnaise, sour cream, Dijon mustard, Country Bob's All Purpose Sauce and salt in a bowl and whisk until well blended. Add the parsley and shallots and mix well. Fold in the whipped cream gently. Chill, covered, for 1 hour or longer. Whisk several times to lighten before serving. Serve as a delicious sauce with steak, roast beef or anything that needs a little zing.

Yield: $2^{1}/2$ cups

We Believe

And this is love: that we walk in obedience
to his commands. As you have heard
from the beginning, his command is that
you walk in love.

2 John 1:6

Country Bob's Corned Beef Cheese Ball

12 ounces corned beef
8 ounces cream cheese, softened
6 green onions, finely chopped
3 tablespoons Country Bob's All Purpose Sauce
1 1/2 teaspoons Worcestershire sauce
1 cup chopped pecans

Cut the corned beef into slivers. Reserve 1/4 cup. Combine the cream cheese with the remaining corned beef, green onions, Country Bob's All Purpose Sauce and Worcestershire sauce and mix well. Mix in the pecans. Shape the mixture into a ball and roll in the reserved corned beef slivers. Chill until serving time. Serve with assorted crackers.

Yield: variable

We Believe

Dear friend, I pray that you may enjoy good health and that all may go well with you, even as your soul is getting along well.

3 John 1:2

Little Party Bites

1 pound Little Smokies
1 tablespoon grated or diced onion (optional)
2 cups Country Bob's All Purpose Sauce

Brown the sausages lightly on all sides in a large skillet. Remove the sausages to paper towels and drain the skillet. Add the onion to the skillet and sauté for 1 minute. Stir in Country Bob's All Purpose Sauce. Return the sausages to the skillet, turning to coat with the sauce. Simmer until heated to serving temperature.

Yield: 4 to 8 servings

We Believe
No, in all these things we are more than conquerors through him who loved us. For I am convinced that neither death nor life, neither angels nor demons, neither the present nor the future, nor any powers, neither height nor depth, nor anything else in all creation, will be able to separate us from the love of God that is in Christ Jesus our Lord.

Romans 8:37-39

Polish Sausages WOW!

2 pounds Polish sausages
1 cup Country Bob's All Purpose Sauce
1 (16-ounce) can whole berry cranberry sauce
Salt and pepper to taste

Slice the sausages and brown lightly in a skillet. Drain the sausage and return to the skillet. Add the Country Bob's All Purpose Sauce and cranberry sauce. Bring to a simmer, stirring until the sauce is well mixed. Simmer for 10 minutes, stirring occasionally. Season with salt and pepper. Serve as an appetizer or snack or on hearty bread or rolls as sandwiches.

Yield: variable

We Believe

This is the message we have heard from him and declare to you: God is light; in him there is no darkness at all. If we claim to have fellowship with him yet walk in the darkness, we lie and do not live by the truth. But if we walk in the light, as he is in the light, we have fellowship with one another, and the blood of Jesus, his Son, purifies us from all sin.

1 John 1:5-7

Country Bob's Pickin' Food

2 cups each corn, wheat, bran and rice Chex
2 cups small pretzels
1 cup chopped nuts
1/2 cup (1 stick) margarine
2 tablespoons Country Bob's Seasoning Salt
1/4 cup Country Bob's All Purpose Sauce

Combine the cereals, pretzels and nuts in a large bowl. Melt the margarine in a small saucepan. Blend in the Country Bob's Seasoning Salt and Country Bob's All Purpose Sauce. Pour the margarine mixture over the cereal mixture and mix gently. Spread the mixture in a large shallow baking pan. Bake at 250 degrees for 1 hour, stirring gently every 15 minutes. Spread on paper towels to cool.

Yield: 11 cups

We Believe

No temptation has seized you except what is common to man. And God is faithful; he will not let you be tempted beyond what you can bear. But when you are tempted, he will also provide a way out so that you can stand up under it.

1 Corinthians 10:13

Homemade Beef and Venison Jerky

2 average-size lean beef or venison roasts
1 (13-ounce) bottle Country Bob's All Purpose Sauce
1 (4-ounce) bottle liquid smoke
1 (10-ounce) bottle Worcestershire sauce
1 (5-ounce) bottle Tabasco sauce
$1/2$ cup soy sauce
1 (12-ounce) can root beer
3 tablespoons Country Bob's Seasoning Salt
1 tablespoon fine garlic powder
2 teaspoons brown sugar
2 teaspoons pepper

Cut the roasts into thin slices, about 3/16 inch thick. Trim off and discard any excess fat. Combine Country Bob's All Purpose Sauce, liquid smoke, Worcestershire sauce, Tabasco sauce, soy sauce and root beer in a large bowl or marinating dish and mix well. Add the Country Bob's Seasoning Salt, garlic powder, brown sugar and pepper and mix well. Add the meat slices and stir gently until coated with marinade. Marinate for several hours to overnight. Drain the meat slices and discard the marinade. Arrange the slices on the racks in a dehydrator and follow appliance instructions for drying.

Yield: variable

Pickled Eggs

12 eggs
1/2 cup Country Bob's All Purpose Sauce
1/4 cup salt
1/4 cup cayenne pepper
1 garlic clove, minced
Dillweed to taste
1 bottle Texas Pete peppers
2 to 3 cups vinegar

Hard-cook the eggs in simmering water to cover in a saucepan; cool in cold water and peel. Prepare the pickling mixture by mixing the Country Bob's All Purpose Sauce, salt, cayenne pepper, garlic, dillweed and peppers in a 1-gallon container. Prepare a vinegar and water solution of 3 parts vinegar to 1 part water. Stir about half the vinegar solution into the pickling mixture. Slip the eggs into the mixture. Add enough of the remaining vinegar solution to cover the eggs and mix gently. Chill the eggs in the pickling mixture for 2 days or longer until the desired flavor is obtained. Remove the eggs from the mixture; drain. Place in a covered jar and cover with fresh water. Store in the refrigerator.

Yield: 12 eggs

Mexican Snack Mix

3 tablespoons butter or margarine
2 tablespoons chili powder
1/4 teaspoon garlic salt
1/4 teaspoon onion salt
3 tablespoons Country Bob's All Purpose Sauce
7 cups Crispix cereal
2 cups small corn chips
1/4 cup (1 ounce) grated Parmesan cheese

Melt the butter in a 9×13-inch baking pan. Stir in the chili powder, garlic salt, onion salt and Country Bob's All Purpose Sauce. Add the cereal and corn chips, stirring until coated. Bake at 250 degrees for 15 minutes. Add the Parmesan cheese and stir to coat. Bake for 30 minutes longer, stirring after 15 minutes. Spread on paper towels to cool. Store in an airtight container.

Yield: 9 cups

We Believe
Peacemakers who sow in peace raise a harvest of righteousness.

James 3:18

Country Bob's Shrimp Salad Deluxe

1 cup mayonnaise
1/4 cup Country Bob's All Purpose Sauce
1 tablespoon prepared horseradish
Salt and pepper to taste
3 cups peeled cocktail shrimp, cooked
1 cup chopped celery
3 hard-cooked eggs, chopped
1/4 cup chopped green onions
1/4 dill pickle, chopped

Combine the mayonnaise, Country Bob's All Purpose Sauce, horseradish, salt and pepper in a small bowl and mix well. Combine the shrimp, celery, eggs, green onions and pickle in a large bowl. Add the mayonnaise mixture to the shrimp mixture and toss lightly.

Yield: 6 servings

We Believe
Salvation is found in no one else, for there is no other name under heaven given to men by which we must be saved.

Acts 4:12

Chinese Salad

1 (12- to 16-ounce) bag washed spinach, stems removed and
leaves torn into bite-sized pieces
1 (7-ounce) can water chestnuts, drained and sliced
1 (16-ounce) can bean sprouts, drained
Sweet and Sour Dressing
2 hard-cooked eggs, sliced
5 slices bacon, crisp-fried and crumbled

Combine the spinach with the water chestnuts and bean sprouts in a salad
bowl. Add the desired amount of Sweet and Sour Dressing and toss lightly.
Top with egg slices and bacon and serve immediately.

Yield: 6 to 8 servings

Sweet and Sour Dressing

1/2 cup sugar
1/4 cup vinegar
1/2 cup Country Bob's
All Purpose Sauce

1 small onion, chopped
Salt and pepper to taste
1 cup vegetable oil

Combine the sugar, vinegar and Country Bob's All Purpose Sauce in a small
jar; cover and shake vigorously until the sugar dissolves. Add the onion, salt,
pepper and oil; cover and shake vigorously. Store dressing in the refrigerator.

23

Coleslaw

8 cups coleslaw mix
1 cup chopped green bell pepper
Sour Cream Slaw Dressing

Combine the coleslaw mix and green pepper in a large bowl and toss lightly to mix. Add the Sour Cream Slaw Dressing and toss to mix. Chill until serving time.

Yield: 12 to 16 servings

Sour Cream Slaw Dressing

$^1/_3$ cup sugar
$^1/_4$ cup vinegar
$^1/_3$ cup Country Bob's All Purpose Sauce
$^1/_4$ cup vegetable oil
2 teaspoons celery seeds
Salt and pepper to taste
$^1/_4$ cup sour cream

Stir the sugar and vinegar in a small bowl until the sugar is dissolved. Add the Country Bob's All Purpose Sauce, oil, celery seeds, salt and pepper and blend well. Blend in the sour cream.

Cucumber and Tomato Salad

1 tomato, chopped
1 cucumber, seeded and chopped
1/4 cup thinly sliced red onion
1/4 cup canned kidney beans, drained
1/4 cup croutons
2 tablespoons chopped fresh basil
1/4 cup balsamic vinaigrette salad dressing
2 tablespoons Country Bob's All Purpose Sauce
Salt and pepper to taste

Combine the tomato, cucumber, red onion, kidney beans, croutons and basil in a salad bowl. Blend the balsamic vinaigrette with Country Bob's All Purpose Sauce in a small bowl. Drizzle over the vegetables and toss to mix. Season with salt and pepper and serve immediately.

Yield: 4 to 6 servings

We Believe

For God so loved the world that he gave his one and only Son, that whoever believes in him shall not perish but have eternal life. For God did not send his Son into the world to condemn the world, but to save the world through him.

John 3:16-17

Country Bob's Poppy Seed Dressing

2/3 cup vinegar
1 small to medium onion, coarsely chopped
2 teaspoons salt
2 teaspoons mustard
3/4 cup sugar
2 tablespoons Country Bob's All Purpose Sauce
1 cup vegetable oil
2 tablespoons poppy seeds or celery seeds

Combine the vinegar, onion, salt, mustard and sugar in a blender. Add Country Bob's All Purpose Sauce and process until smooth. Add the oil in a fine stream, processing constantly. Stir in the poppy seeds. Store in the refrigerator.

Yield: 2 1/2 to 3 cups

We Believe
I want to know Christ and the power of his resurrection and the fellowship of sharing in his sufferings, becoming like him in his death, and so, somehow, to attain to the resurrection from the dead.

Philippians 3:10-11

Zesty Sweet and Sour Salad Dressing

1/2 cup vegetable oil

1/3 cup red wine vinegar

2 tablespoons sugar

1/2 teaspoon salt

1/2 teaspoon celery salt

1/2 teaspoon pepper

1/2 teaspoon dry mustard

1 garlic clove, minced

2 tablespoons Country Bob's All Purpose Sauce

1/4 teaspoon Tabasco sauce

Combine the oil, vinegar, sugar, seasonings, garlic, Country Bob's All Purpose Sauce and Tabasco sauce in a jar; cover and shake vigorously. Store in the refrigerator.

Yield: 1 cup

We Believe

May God himself, the God of peace, sanctify you through and through. May your whole spirit, soul and body be kept blameless at the coming of our Lord Jesus Christ. The one who calls you is faithful and he will do it.

1 Thessalonians 5:23-24

Black Bean Soup

8 slices lean bacon
3 (16-ounce) cans black beans
1/3 cup Country Bob's All Purpose Sauce
1 cup chopped onion
3 garlic cloves, minced
1 tablespoon vegetable oil
1 (24-ounce) jar chunky salsa
2 tablespoons lime juice
1 teaspoon ground cumin
1/2 teaspoon crushed red pepper
1/2 cup plain yogurt

Cook the bacon until crisp; drain well. Crumble and set aside. Process the beans with the bean liquid and Country Bob's All Purpose Sauce in a food processor or blender until smooth. Sauté the onion and garlic in the oil in a large saucepan until tender. Add the bean mixture, salsa, lime juice, cumin and red pepper and mix well. Simmer, covered, for 25 to 30 minutes, stirring occasionally. Ladle into soup bowls. Top each serving with a dollop of yogurt and sprinkle with crisp bacon.

Yield: 6 to 8 servings

Olivia's Egg Drop Soup

2 cups water
1 bouillon cube
2 eggs
1 teaspoon Country Bob's All Purpose Sauce
1/4 teaspoon Country Bob's Seasoning Salt

Bring the water with the bouillon cube to a boil in a medium saucepan. Beat the eggs with Country Bob's All Purpose Sauce and Country Bob's Seasoning Salt in a small bowl. Stir the hot bouillon with a chopstick or fork in a brisk circular motion to resemble a whirlpool. Pour the egg mixture into the center gradually while continuing to stir. The egg will cook instantly, forming tender strands. Ladle into soup bowls and serve immediately.

Yield: 2 servings

We Believe

He said to them, "Go into all the world and preach the good news to all creation. Whoever believes and is baptized will be saved, but whoever does not believe will be condemned."

Mark 16:15-16

Country Bob's Onion Soup

1 large onion, chopped
1/2 teaspoon Country Bob's Seasoning Salt
2 tablespoons olive oil
1 teaspoon balsamic vinegar
6 cups water
2 beef bouillon cubes
2 tablespoons Country Bob's Spicy Hot All Purpose Sauce
1/2 teaspoon chopped rosemary leaves
4 slices crusty bread
1/2 cup (2 ounces) shredded mozzarella cheese

Sauté the onion with Country Bob's Seasoning Salt in the olive oil in a skillet until golden brown. Stir in the balsamic vinegar. Bring the water with the bouillon cubes to a boil in a large saucepan. Stir in the Country Bob's Spicy Hot All Purpose Sauce, sautéed onion and rosemary. Simmer, covered, for 30 minutes. Sprinkle the bread with mozzarella cheese and broil until golden and bubbly. Ladle the soup into bowls and float a slice of the bread on top. Note: May substitute Country Bob's All Purpose Sauce plus 6 drops of Tabasco sauce for the Country Bob's Spicy Hot All Purpose Sauce.

Yield: 4 servings

Country Potato Soup

8 slices bacon, chopped
1/4 cup chopped celery
1/2 cup chopped onion
2 medium potatoes
2 1/2 cups water
1 bay leaf
1/4 teaspoon nutmeg
1/4 teaspoon dried marjoram
1/4 teaspoon celery salt
1/4 teaspoon black pepper
1 cup milk
1/4 cup Country Bob's All Purpose Sauce
2 tablespoons minced fresh parsley
1 bunch green onions, chopped

Sauté the bacon, celery and onion in a large soup pot until the onion is golden. Peel the potatoes and cut into 1-inch cubes. Add to the pot with the water and seasonings. Simmer, covered, for 15 minutes or until the potatoes are tender. Remove the bay leaf. Mash the potatoes slightly, leaving some chunks. Stir in the milk, Country Bob's All Purpose Sauce and parsley. Heat to serving temperature. Ladle into soup bowls and sprinkle with chopped green onions.

Yield: 4 to 6 servings

Grilling

We Believe

...that the Bible is the inspired word of God—
a lamp unto our feet and a
light unto our path.

(2 Timothy 3:16 and Psalm 119:105)

All-Purpose Marinade or Basting Sauce

1 cup vegetable oil
$1/4$ cup soy sauce
$1/2$ cup vinegar
$2/3$ cup Country Bob's All Purpose Sauce
2 tablespoons dry mustard
1 teaspoon salt
1 tablespoon pepper
2 teaspoons chopped fresh parsley
$1/2$ teaspoon garlic powder
$1/2$ to 1 teaspoon Tabasco sauce (optional)

Combine the oil, soy sauce, vinegar, Country Bob's All Purpose Sauce, dry mustard, salt, pepper, parsley, garlic powder and Tabasco sauce in a blender and process until the parsley is puréed. Use as desired for preparing beef, venison or chicken. For best grilling flavor: Marinate the beef, venison or chicken in a portion of the marinade in the refrigerator for 2 to 4 hours. Drain and discard the marinade. Place the beef, venison or chicken on the grill over hot coals and cook to the desired degree of doneness, turning and basting frequently with the remaining marinade. Chicken should be grilled until its juices run clear when pierced with a fork.

Yield: $2^{1/2}$ cups

Country Bob's Teriyaki Grill

3 cups vinaigrette salad dressing
1 cup Worcestershire sauce
3 cups Country Bob's All Purpose Sauce
1 cup Dijon mustard
1 cup packed brown sugar
1/3 cup ground ginger
2 tablespoons garlic powder
10 pounds steak or chicken
Mixed salad greens

Combine the salad dressing, Worcestershire sauce and Country Bob's All Purpose Sauce in a large bowl. Add the mustard, brown sugar, ginger and garlic powder and mix well. Store in the refrigerator. Place the steaks in a large pan. Reserve 3 cups of the marinade to use as the dressing. Pour the remaining marinade over the steaks, turning to coat. Cover and marinate in the refrigerator for 3 hours to overnight. Remove the steaks from the marinade, reserving the marinade for basting. Place the steaks on the grill over hot coals. Grill steaks until medium rare, turning and basting frequently with the reserved marinade. Do not baste during the last 5 minutes of grilling. Let rest for 15 minutes before slicing. Slice the steak cross grain as desired. Line plates with mixed salad greens and arrange steak over the top. Drizzle each serving with 1 ounce of the reserved dressing.

Yield: variable

Marinated Beef Skewers

1/2 cup (1 stick) melted margarine
1 cup olive oil
1 cup cider vinegar
1/2 cup lime juice
1/4 cup Country Bob's All Purpose Sauce
1 tablespoon salt
1 teaspoon white pepper
1/2 teaspoon cayenne pepper
1 garlic clove, minced
1 teaspoon dried mint
4 pounds boneless top sirloin

Prepare the marinade by mixing the margarine, olive oil, vinegar, lime juice, Country Bob's All Purpose Sauce, salt, white pepper, cayenne pepper, garlic and mint in a large glass dish. Discard excess fat from sirloin and cut into 1-inch cubes. Place cubes in the marinade and stir to coat. Marinate in the refrigerator for 4 hours. Remove the steak cubes from the marinade, reserving the marinade. Thread the steak cubes onto skewers. Grill over medium-hot coals, basting with the reserved marinade and turning every 5 minutes.

Yield: variable

Poor Man's Fillet

6 slices bacon
2 pounds ground sirloin or lean ground beef
1/2 cup finely chopped onion
1 teaspoon minced garlic
Salt and pepper to taste
1/4 cup Country Bob's All Purpose Sauce
1 cup (4 ounces) shredded mild Cheddar cheese
4 slices bacon

Cook 6 slices bacon until crisp. Drain, crumble and set aside. Combine the ground sirloin, chopped onion, garlic, salt, pepper and Country Bob's All Purpose Sauce in a large bowl and mix thoroughly. Add 1/2 cup of the shredded cheese to the mixture, mixing well. Shape into 8 patties about the thickness of a hamburger patty. Divide the crumbled bacon and the remaining 1/2 cup shredded cheese into 4 equal amounts. Place on 4 of the patties. Sprinkle each of the 4 patties lightly with additional Country Bob's All Purpose Sauce if desired. Top with the remaining patties. Press the edges tightly all around to seal. Wrap each fillet with the bacon slices around the edge and secure the bacon with a wooden or metal pick. Place on the grill over hot coals. Grill until cooked through, turning several times and basting with additional Country Bob's All Purpose Sauce.

Yield: 4 servings

Country Bob's Super Burgers

(Winner "Best of Show" in St. Louis BBQ Cookoff)

2 1/2 pounds lean ground beef
1/2 envelope onion soup mix
6 tablespoons Country Bob's All Purpose Sauce
1 tablespoon Country Bob's Seasoning Salt
6 to 10 tablespoons Country Bob's All Purpose Sauce

Combine the ground beef, onion soup mix, Country Bob's All Purpose Sauce and Country Bob's Seasoning Salt in a bowl and mix well. Divide into 6 to 10 portions and shape into patties of the desired thickness. Grill over hot coals until cooked through. Top each with 1 tablespoon Country Bob's All Purpose Sauce. Serve as desired.

Yield: 6 to 10 servings

We Believe

For the word of God is living and active. Sharper than any double-edged sword, it penetrates even to dividing soul and spirit, joints and marrow; it judges the thought and attitudes of the heart.

Hebrews 4:12

Honolulu Bob Burgers

2 pounds ground beef
Country Bob's All Purpose Sauce
4 well-drained canned pineapple slices
4 slices Cheddar cheese

Divide the ground beef into 4 portions and shape each into a patty. Grill over hot coals until cooked on one side. Turn the patties over. Spread with the desired amount of Country Bob's All Purpose Sauce and top with the pineapple slices. Grill for several minutes or until cooked through. Add the cheese slices. Grill until the cheese melts. Top with additional Country Bob's All Purpose Sauce and serve as desired.

Yield: 4 servings

We Believe

You are the light of the world. A city on a hill cannot be hidden. Neither do people light a lamp and put it under a bowl. Instead, they put it on its stand, and it gives light to everyone in the house. In the same way, let your light shine before men, that they may see your good deeds and praise your Father in Heaven.

Matthew 5:14-16

Camping Silver Treasure Chests

Ground beef patties
Onion slices
Fresh carrot slices
Potato slices
Butter
Salt and pepper to taste
Country Bob's All Purpose Sauce

Prepare as many Treasure Chests as needed: Place 1 ground beef patty, 1 onion slice, several carrot slices and several potato slices on a large square of heavy-duty foil. Add a pat of butter, sprinkle with salt and pepper to taste and top with 1 1/2 tablespoons Country Bob's All Purpose Sauce. Bring the edges of the foil together and seal tightly. Place on hot coals or on a grill over hot coals. Cook for 30 minutes on each side or until cooked through. Packets may also be baked in the oven. Vary the vegetables as desired.

Yield: variable

We Believe
God made him who had no sin to be sin for us, so that in him we might become the righteousness of God.

2 Corinthians 5:21

Grilled Pork Tenderloins

2 large whole pork tenderloins
1 cup soy sauce
1/3 cup sesame oil
3 garlic cloves, minced

1 tablespoon ground ginger
1 (13-ounce) bottle Country Bob's
All Purpose Sauce
Finishing Touch Sauce (below)

Place pork tenderloins in a shallow glass dish. Mix the soy sauce, sesame oil, garlic, ginger and Country Bob's All Purpose Sauce together. Pour over the tenderloins. Marinate, covered, in the refrigerator for about 4 hours, turning every hour. Drain, reserving the marinade. Place the tenderloins in a covered grill over low coals. Grill for about 2 hours, brushing with the reserved marinade about every 15 minutes. Discard any remaining marinade. Grill for 30 minutes longer, brushing occasionally with several tablespoons of Finishing Touch Sauce. Let rest before slicing and serve with the remaining Finishing Touch Sauce.

Yield: 6 to 10 servings

Finishing Touch Sauce

1 (13-ounce) bottle Country Bob's
All Purpose Sauce
1/2 cup soy sauce

1/4 cup sesame oil
1 tablespoon ground ginger

Combine all the ingredients in a bowl and mix well. Store, covered, in the refrigerator.

Really Tender Pork Ribs, Steaks or Chops

Pork ribs, steaks or chops
Coury Bob's Seasoning Salt

Country Bob's All Purpose Sauce

Place the pork on large sheets of foil. Sprinkle with Country Bob's Seasoning Salt to taste and seal tightly. Place on the the grill away from direct heat for about 50 minutes to tenderize. Unwrap, dip in Country Bob's All Purpose Sauce and grill over hot coals for 10 minutes or until cooked through.

Yield: variable

Venison Steaks

3 pounds venison loin steaks
1 cup Country Bob's
All Purpose Sauce
3 tablespoons roasted garlic-
flavored olive oil

2 tablespoons powdered garlic
1 tablespoon teriyaki sauce
Onion salt to taste
Seasoned pepper to taste

Place the venison and a mixture of the remaining ingredients in a plastic bag and seal. Chill for 2 hours or longer. Let stand at room temperature for about 1 hour. Grill over hot coals until cooked through, turning and basting frequently.

Yield: 8 to 12 servings

Huli Huli Chicken

1/3 cup Country Bob's All Purpose Sauce
1/4 cup soy sauce
1/2 cup chicken broth
3 tablespoons frozen pineapple juice concentrate, thawed
1 teaspoon minced fresh ginger or garlic
3 chicken breasts

Mix the Country Bob's All Purpose Sauce, soy sauce, chicken broth, pineapple juice concentrate and ginger in a glass dish. Add the chicken to the mixture, turning to coat. Marinate in the refrigerator for 24 hours, turning occasionally. Drain the chicken, discarding the marinade. Place the chicken on the grill over low to medium-hot coals. Grill until juices run clear when pierced with a fork, turning occasionally. Do not overcook.

Yield: 3 servings

We Believe

Give, and it will be given to you. A good measure, pressed down, shaken together and running over, will be poured into your lap. For with the measure you use, it will be measured to you.

Luke 6:38

Foil-Wrapped Chicken

1 (14-ounce) can baby corn, drained
2 carrots, sliced
8 chicken thighs or 4 chicken breasts, skinned
2 green onions, sliced
1 tablespoon sesame seeds, toasted
1/3 cup soy sauce
3 tablespoons hoisin sauce
1 tablespoon minced fresh ginger
1 garlic clove, pressed
1/2 cup Country Bob's All Purpose Sauce

Cut four 12×18-inch pieces of heavy-duty foil. Place equal portions of the corn and carrots in the center of each sheet and top each with 2 chicken thighs or a chicken breast. Sprinkle with green onions. Mix 2 teaspoons of the sesame seeds, soy sauce, hoisin sauce, ginger, garlic and Country Bob's All Purpose Sauce in a bowl. Spoon evenly over the chicken. Bring up 2 sides of each foil sheet and double fold with folds about 1 inch wide. Double fold each end to form a packet, sealing but leaving room for heat circulation inside. Grill, covered with grill lid, over medium-high heat, 350 to 400 degrees, for about 35 minutes or until the chicken is cooked through. Open the foil and sprinkle with the remaining 1 teaspoon sesame seeds.

Yield: 4 servings

Grilled Chicken-in-a-Pocket

4 boneless skinless chicken breasts
1 cup Country Bob's All Purpose Sauce
4 large mushrooms, thinly sliced
1/2 small onion, thinly sliced
1 small zucchini, thinly sliced

Cut four 10×12-inch pieces of heavy-duty foil. Place a chicken breast in the center of each. Top each chicken breast with 1/4 cup Country Bob's All Purpose Sauce and 1/4 of the mushrooms, onion and zucchini. Fold the edges of the foil together to seal each packet. Place the packets on the grill over hot coals. Grill for 20 to 30 minutes or until the chicken and vegetables are cooked through, turning the packets occasionally.

Yield: 4 servings

We Believe

To him who is able to keep you from falling and to present you before his glorious presence without fault and with great joy—to the only God our Savior be glory, majesty, power, and authority, through Jesus Christ our Lord, before all ages, now and forevermore! Amen.

Jude 1:24-25

Brat Stuffer

2 large bell peppers
2 medium onions
1/4 cup Country Bob's
All Purpose Sauce

1 teaspoon pepper
1/4 teaspoon ground lemon peel
2 tablespoons brown sugar
Grilled bratwursts

Cut the peppers into thin strips and cut the onions into small pieces. Place in a saucepan. Add the Country Bob's All Purpose Sauce, pepper and lemon peel. Heat to a simmer and then add brown sugar. Simmer until the vegetables are cooked to taste. Serve over grilled bratwursts.

Yield: 2 to 3 cups

We Believe

For the grace of God that brings salvation has appeared to all men. It teaches us to say, "No," to ungodliness and worldly passions, and to live self-controlled, upright and godly lives in this present age, while we wait for the blessed hope— the glorious appearing of our great God and Savior, Jesus Christ, who gave himself for us to redeem us from all wickedness and to purify for himself a people that are his very own, eager to do what is good.

Titus 2:11-14

Famous Grilled Cauliflower

1 large head cauliflower
1/4 cup (1/2 stick) butter or margarine
1 tablespoon Country Bob's Seasoning Salt
2 tablespoons grated Parmesan cheese

Remove the green leaves from the cauliflower. Place the whole cauliflower on a large sheet of heavy-duty foil. Rub butter or margarine over the entire cauliflower head. Sprinkle with Country Bob's Seasoning Salt and Parmesan cheese. Wrap the cauliflower in the foil. Place on the grill over medium-hot coals. Grill for 30 minutes or until cooked to the desired tenderness.

Yield: variable

We Believe

Therefore, my brothers, be all the more eager to make your calling and election sure. For if you do these things, you will never fall, and you will receive a rich welcome into the eternal kingdom of our Lord and Savior Jesus Christ.

2 Peter 1:10-11

Main Dishes

We Believe

...that every person has worth as a creation of God, but that all have sinned and fallen short of the glory of God.

(Romans 3:23)

...that forgiveness of sins and the promise of eternal life are available to those who trust Christ as Savior and Lord.

(John 3:16)

...that those accepting Christ should repent of sin, confess their faith, and be baptized into Him.

(Romans 10:9 and Acts 2:38)

Country Bob's Meat Loaf

1 1/2 pounds lean ground beef
1/4 cup chopped onion
12 saltine crackers, crushed
2 eggs, beaten
3/4 cup Country Bob's All Purpose Sauce
1/4 cup milk
1 tablespoon Country Bob's Seasoning Salt
1/4 teaspoon pepper

Combine the ground beef, onion, cracker crumbs, eggs, Country Bob's All Purpose Sauce, milk, Country Bob's Seasoning Salt and pepper in a bowl and mix well. Shape into a loaf and place in a baking pan. Spread the desired amount of additional Country Bob's All Purpose Sauce on top of the loaf. Bake at 350 degrees for 1 hour or until the loaf is cooked through. Remove the loaf to a serving plate. Let stand for several minutes before slicing.

Yield: 6 to 8 servings

We Believe

And whatever you do, whether in word or deed, do it all in the name of the Lord Jesus, giving thanks to God the Father through him.

Colossians 3:17

Sweet and Sour Pot Roast

1 (3-pound) beef roast
1 tablespoon vegetable oil
12 small potatoes, peeled
1 cup chopped onion
1 (15-ounce) can tomato sauce
1/4 cup packed brown sugar
1/2 cup Country Bob's All Purpose Sauce
2 tablespoons cider vinegar
1 teaspoon salt

Trim fat from the roast. Brown the roast in hot oil in a skillet on all sides. Place the potatoes in a slow cooker. Place the browned roast on the potatoes. Discard all but 1 tablespoon drippings from the skillet. Sauté the onion in the drippings until tender. Stir in the tomato sauce, brown sugar, Country Bob's All Purpose Sauce, vinegar and salt. Pour over the roast and potatoes. Cover and cook on High for 4 to 5 hours or until the roast is tender. Remove the roast and potatoes to a serving platter. Pour the sauce into a skillet. Cook over medium heat until thickened to the desired consistency, stirring frequently. Serve with the potatoes and roast.

Yield: 8 to 12 servings

Savory Swiss Steak

1 1/2 pounds round steak
1/4 cup flour
1 teaspoon dry mustard
1 teaspoon salt
1/4 teaspoon pepper
1 tablespoon each vinegar and
lemon juice
2 tablespoons soy sauce

1 tablespoon butter
2 tablespoons vegetable oil
1 onion, finely chopped
2 carrots, peeled and grated
2 ribs celery, finely chopped
1/2 cup Country Bob's
All Purpose Sauce
1/4 cup packed brown sugar

Cut the steak into 6 serving-size pieces. Mix the flour, mustard, salt, pepper, vinegar, lemon juice and soy sauce in a shallow dish. Coat the steak pieces with the mixture. Heat half the butter and oil in a skillet and brown the steak on both sides. Place in a slow cooker. Sauté the onion, carrots and celery in the remaining butter and oil in the skillet until glazed. Add the Country Bob's All Purpose Sauce and brown sugar. Heat and stir to deglaze the skillet. Pour over the steak. Cook, covered, on Low for 6 to 8 hours or until tender. Serve the steaks with the sauce. Garnish with parsley.

Yield: 6 servings

Country Bob's French Dip Sandwiches

1 (3-pound) beef roast
1 (14-ounce) can beef broth
1 cup Country Bob's All Purpose Sauce
2 teaspoons Country Bob's Seasoning Salt
1/2 teaspoon ground rosemary
1 teaspoon garlic powder
1/2 teaspoon pepper
1 bay leaf
Hearty bread or rolls

Remove fat from the roast and place in a slow cooker. Combine the broth, Country Bob's All Purpose Sauce, Country Bob's Seasoning Salt, rosemary, garlic powder, pepper and bay leaf in a bowl and mix well. Pour over the roast. Add enough water to almost cover the roast. Cover and cook on Low for 10 to 12 hours or until the roast is very tender. Remove the roast from the broth and shred with a fork. Reserve the broth. Discard the bay leaf. Heat the broth. Make sandwiches of the bread and shredded roast. Serve with individual bowls of the broth for dipping.

Yield: variable

Hungarian Goulash

2 pounds beef roast
1 large onion, sliced
1 garlic clove, minced
3/4 cup Country Bob's All Purpose Sauce
2 teaspoons salt
2 teaspoons paprika
1/2 teaspoon dry mustard
1 cup water
1/2 cup flour
Hot cooked noodles or rice

Cube the roast and place in a slow cooker. Cover with sliced onion. Combine the garlic, Country Bob's All Purpose Sauce, salt, paprika and mustard in a bowl. Add the water and mix well. Pour over the roast and onion. Cover and cook on Low for 9 to 10 hours. Turn the control to High. Blend the flour with a small amount of cold water. Stir into the beef mixture. Cook, uncovered, on High for 10 to 15 minutes or until slightly thickened, stirring frequently. Serve the goulash over hot cooked noodles or rice.

Yield: 8 to 10 servings

Sour Cream Meat Loaf

1 1/2 cups sour cream
2 green onions, chopped
1/4 cup Country Bob's All Purpose Sauce
1 (3-ounce) can sliced mushrooms, drained
2 pounds lean ground beef
1 1/2 cups soft bread crumbs
2 eggs
1/4 cup milk
2 teaspoons salt

Combine the sour cream, green onions, Country Bob's All Purpose Sauce and mushrooms in a small bowl. Mix well and set aside. Combine the ground beef, bread crumbs, eggs, milk and salt in a large bowl and mix well. Shape the mixture into a long 4-inch wide rectangle in an ungreased shallow baking dish. Make a 2-inch-deep well lengthwise down the center of the loaf. Spoon the sour cream mixture into the well. Leave the sour cream mixture exposed. Bake at 350 degrees for 1 to 1 1/4 hours or until the loaf is cooked through. Remove the loaf to a serving plate. Variation: Substitute ground chicken or turkey for the ground beef.

Yield: 8 servings

Country Bob's Steak Taco

Grilled steak
Flour tortillas, warmed
Country Bob's All Purpose Sauce
Cheddar cheese, shredded
Lettuce, shredded

This super-easy recipe is suitable for just one person or a thundering herd of hungry teenagers. Just have enough fixings ready. Grill the steak to taste and cut into thin slices. Divide the steak slices among the warm flour tortillas. Add Country Bob's All Purpose Sauce, cheese and lettuce and fold over or roll the tortillas to enclose the filling.

Yield: variable

We Believe

I have been crucified with Christ and I no longer live, but Christ lives in me. The life I live in the body, I live by faith in the Son of God, who loved me and gave himself for me.

Galatians 2:20

Country Bob's Thirty-Minute Chili Mac

1 pound ground beef
1/2 cup chopped onion
1 (16-ounce) can crushed tomatoes
1/4 cup chopped green bell pepper (optional)
1/4 cup Country Bob's All Purpose Sauce
2 tablespoons chili powder
2 cups macaroni
1/4 cup chopped green onions
1/4 cup (1 ounce) shredded Cheddar cheese

Cook the ground beef with the onion in a skillet over medium heat until brown and crumbly; drain. Add the tomatoes, green pepper, Country Bob's All Purpose Sauce and chili powder and mix well. Bring to a simmer and cook, covered, for 10 minutes. Cook the macaroni according to the package directions and drain well. Stir the macaroni into the skillet and sprinkle with the green onions and cheese.

Yield: 4 servings

Corn Pone Pie

1 pound ground beef
$1/3$ cup chopped onion
1 tablespoon shortening
1 cup stewed tomatoes
1 cup Country Bob's All Purpose Sauce
2 tablespoons chili powder
$3/4$ teaspoon salt
1 (16-ounce) can kidney beans
1 (6-ounce) package corn bread mix

Cook the ground beef with the onion in the shortening in a skillet until brown and crumbly; drain. Stir in the tomatoes, Country Bob's All Purpose Sauce, chili powder and salt. Simmer, covered, for about 15 minutes. Discard about half the bean liquid. Stir the beans with the remaining liquid into the skillet. Pour the mixture into a greased casserole. Prepare the corn bread mix according to the package directions. Pour the batter over the ground beef mixture. Bake at 425 degrees for 20 minutes or until golden brown.

Yield: 6 servings

Down Home Steak

2 to 4 tablespoons butter
7 pounds (about) potatoes
2 (10-ounce) cans cream of mushroom soup
2/3 cup water
Country Bob's All Purpose Sauce to taste
6 to 10 pieces lean tender steak
Salt and pepper to taste

Melt the butter in a 9×13-inch baking pan. Peel the potatoes and cut into 1-inch pieces. Mix the soups with the water in a bowl. Layer half the potatoes, half the soup mixture and Country Bob's All Purpose Sauce in the prepared pan. Arrange the steak pieces over the potato layer. Repeat the layers with the remaining potatoes, soup mixture and Country Bob's All Purpose Sauce. Sprinkle with salt and pepper. Cover the pan tightly with foil. Bake at 350 degrees for 1 hour or until the potatoes and steak are tender.

Yield: 6 to 8 servings

Deluxe Stuffed Hoagies

5 hoagie rolls or 1 loaf French bread
1 pound lean ground beef
1 medium onion, chopped
$1/2$ (10-ounce) can tomato soup
1 (10-ounce) can Cheddar cheese soup
1 cup Country Bob's All Purpose Sauce
$1/2$ teaspoon Country Bob's Seasoning Salt
$1/2$ cup chopped green bell pepper

Slice the rolls or bread horizontally lengthwise into halves. Scoop out the centers carefully to form shells and tear the scooped-out bread into pieces. Set the bread shells and pieces aside. Cook the ground beef with the onion in a skillet until brown and crumbly; drain. Stir in the tomato and cheese soups, Country Bob's All Purpose Sauce, Country Bob's Seasoning Salt, green pepper and the bread pieces. Cook until heated through. Spoon the mixture into the bottom shells and cover with the tops. Wrap individually in foil. Bake at 350 degrees for 30 minutes. Unwrap carefully. Place on a serving platter and cut into portions.

Yield: 5 servings

Coney Island Hot Dog Sauce

1 pound ground beef
1 medium onion, diced
2 tablespoons prepared mustard
2 tablespoons vinegar
2 tablespoons sugar
2 tablespoons water
1/4 teaspoon celery seeds
1/3 cup (or more) Country Bob's All Purpose Sauce

Cook the ground beef with the onion in a skillet until brown and crumbly; drain well. Add the mustard, vinegar, sugar, water and celery seeds and mix well. Add enough Country Bob's All Purpose Sauce to make the mixture the desired consistency. Simmer, loosely covered, for several minutes, stirring occasionally and adding additional Country Bob's All Purpose Sauce as necessary.

Yield: enough for 8 hot dogs

Super Sloppy Joes

1 1/2 pounds ground beef
1/2 cup chopped onion
1 cup diced celery
1 green bell pepper, diced
1 garlic clove, minced
6 slices bacon, crisp-fried
and crumbled
1 (6-ounce) can tomato paste
3/4 cup water

3/4 cup Country Bob's
All Purpose Sauce
1 teaspoon salt
1/8 teaspoon pepper
1/2 teaspoon paprika
2 tablespoons white vinegar
2 teaspoons brown sugar
1 teaspoon dry mustard
Hamburger buns, toasted

Cook the ground beef in a skillet until brown and crumbly; drain. Combine with the onion, celery, green pepper, garlic and bacon in a slow cooker. Add the tomato paste, water, Country Bob's All Purpose Sauce, salt, pepper, paprika, vinegar, brown sugar and mustard and mix well. Cover and cook on Low for 6 to 8 hours. Serve on toasted hamburger buns or as a main dish over hot cooked rice or noodles.

Yield: 8 to 10 servings

Southwestern Black Bean Stew

1 1/2 pounds ground beef
1 envelope taco seasoning mix
1 (15-ounce) can whole kernel corn, drained
1 (15-ounce) can black beans
1 (6-ounce) can tomato paste
1 1/4 cups water
1/4 cup Country Bob's All Purpose Sauce
1/2 cup sour cream
4 cups (16 ounces) shredded Cheddar cheese

Cook the ground beef in a large skillet until brown and crumbly; drain. Add the taco seasoning mix according to the package directions and simmer for 10 minutes. Combine the drained corn, undrained black beans, tomato paste, water and Country Bob's All Purpose Sauce in a slow cooker. Stir in the ground beef mixture. Cover and cook on Low for 5 to 6 hours. Stir in the sour cream. Cook on High for 15 to 20 minutes; do not allow the mixture to boil. Ladle into soup bowls and top with the cheese.

Yield: 8 to 10 servings

Black Bean Stir-Fry Chili

1 pound ground beef
2 garlic cloves, minced
2 medium green bell peppers, coarsely chopped
1 large onion, chopped
Vegetable oil
2 medium zucchini, coarsely chopped
2 cups frozen whole kernel corn
$1/2$ teaspoon each chili powder and salt
$1/4$ teaspoon pepper
$1/4$ cup Country Bob's All Purpose Sauce
1 (15-ounce) can black beans, rinsed and drained
1 (14-ounce) can tomatoes
1 (8-ounce) can tomato sauce
1 jalapeño pepper, seeded and minced
2 cups hot cooked couscous or rice

Cook the ground beef in a wok or large skillet until brown and crumbly. Add the garlic, green peppers and onion and stir-fry for 3 minutes. Remove to a bowl. Add a small amount of vegetable oil to the wok and stir-fry the zucchini and corn for 2 minutes. Add the chili powder, salt, pepper and Country Bob's All Purpose Sauce. Stir-fry for 2 minutes or until the vegetables are tender-crisp. Combine the remaining ingredients in a large saucepan. Stir the ground beef and all the vegetables into the bean mixture. Simmer for 25 minutes, stirring frequently.

Yield: 12 to 15 servings

Down Home Chili

4 pounds lean ground beef
1 tablespoon (rounded) chopped garlic
1/2 cup vegetable oil
2 1/2 tablespoons ground cumin
2 tablespoons chili powder
1 tablespoon salt
1/2 teaspoon pepper
3 (10-ounce) cans tomato soup
3 cups water
3 (20-ounce) cans chili hot beans
1/2 cup Country Bob's All Purpose Sauce

Cook the ground beef and garlic in the oil in a large soup pot over medium-low heat until brown and crumbly. Add the seasonings. Cook for 15 minutes, stirring frequently. Add the soups, water, beans and Country Bob's All Purpose Sauce and mix well. Simmer, covered, for 50 minutes, stirring occasionally. Ladle into soup bowls and garnish with a sprinkle of shredded Cheddar cheese. This chili freezes well if there is any left.

Yield: 10 servings

Taco Soup

1 1/2 pounds lean ground beef or ground turkey
1 onion, chopped
2 (10-ounce) cans tomatoes with green chiles
1 (15-ounce) can kidney beans, drained
1 (15-ounce) can white hominy, drained
1 envelope taco seasoning mix
1 envelope ranch dressing mix
1/4 cup Country Bob's All Purpose Sauce
1 1/4 cups (or more) water
1/4 cup (1 ounce) shredded Cheddar cheese
1/4 cup sour cream

Cook the ground beef with the onion in a Dutch oven until brown and crumbly; drain. Add the tomatoes with green chiles, kidney beans, hominy, taco seasoning mix and ranch dressing mix and mix well. Stir in Country Bob's All Purpose Sauce and 1 1/4 cups water. Simmer for 2 hours, stirring frequently and adding 1 to 2 cups water to make the soup of the desired consistency. Ladle into soup bowls and top with cheese and sour cream.

Yield: 8 servings

Country Bob's Venison Mexican Pizza

1 (8-ounce) package corn
bread mix
1 pound ground venison or ground beef
1 onion, chopped
$1/2$ green bell pepper, chopped
1 envelope taco seasoning mix
$1/2$ cup Country Bob's Spicy Hot All Purpose Sauce
2 cups (8 ounces) shredded Cheddar cheese

Prepare the corn bread mix according to the package directions. Spread the batter in a greased 12-inch pizza pan. Bake at 400 degrees for 9 minutes or until lightly browned. Cook the venison with the onion and green pepper in a skillet until brown and crumbly. Mix in the taco seasoning mix and Country Bob's Spicy Hot All Purpose Sauce. Layer half the cheese, all the venison mixture and the remaining cheese over the corn bread crust. Bake for 5 minutes or until the cheese melts. Top the pizza with any combination of favorite toppings, such as shredded lettuce, chopped tomato, salsa and sour cream. May substitute Country Bob's All Purpose Sauce mixed with $1/4$ teaspoon cayenne pepper for Country Bob's Spicy Hot All Purpose Sauce.

Yield: 6 servings

Country Bob's Rice and Pork

2 pounds lean pork
1 medium green bell pepper
1 medium onion
2 tablespoons butter or margarine
4 cups quick-cooking rice
4 cups water
1 (28-ounce) can peaches
2 cups Country Bob's All Purpose Sauce
Salt and pepper to taste

Cut the pork into cubes. Chop the green pepper and onion into the desired size pieces. Cook the pork and vegetables in the butter in a large skillet or Dutch oven until lightly browned on all sides. Stir in the rice and water. Bring to a boil and reduce the heat. Cover and cook for 15 to 20 minutes or until the rice is cooked through. Drain the peaches, reserving the juice; cut the peaches into bite-sized pieces. Add the peaches, peach juice and Country Bob's All Purpose Sauce to the pork mixture, mixing gently. Season with salt and pepper. Heat to serving temperature.

Yield: 8 to 10 servings

Spicy Chicken Pizza

2 cups chopped chicken
1/4 cup Country Bob's All Purpose Sauce
1/4 cup Country Bob's Barbecue Sauce
1 package pizza crust mix, prepared
1 1/2 cups (6 ounces) shredded Cojack cheese
1/2 green bell pepper, thinly sliced
1/2 sweet onion, thinly sliced

Marinate the chicken in a mixture of Country Bob's All Purpose Sauce and Country Bob's Barbecue Sauce in the refrigerator for 1 hour to overnight. Drain the chicken, discarding the marinade. Stir-fry the chicken in a skillet or wok until cooked through. Set aside. Pat the pizza dough into a pizza pan dusted generously with cornmeal. Sprinkle with 1 cup of the cheese. Add layers of the chicken, the remaining 1/2 cup cheese, green pepper and onion. Bake at 425 degrees for 15 to 20 minutes or until the crust is golden brown.

Yield: 2 to 4 servings

Chicken à la Great

1 (6-ounce) can frozen lemonade concentrate, thawed
$1/2$ cup honey
1 teaspoon pepper
1 teaspoon sage
$1/2$ teaspoon ground mustard
$1/2$ teaspoon dried thyme
$1/2$ teaspoon lemon juice
$1/3$ cup Country Bob's All Purpose Sauce
8 boneless skinless chicken breasts ($2^{1}/2$ pounds)

Combine the lemonade concentrate with the honey, pepper, sage, ground mustard, thyme, lemon juice and Country Bob's All Purpose Sauce in a bowl and mix well. Place the chicken in a shallow baking dish sprayed with nonstick cooking spray. Pour the lemonade mixture over the chicken, turning to coat. Marinate in the refrigerator for 30 minutes. Spoon the lemonade mixture over the chicken. Bake, uncovered, at 350 degrees for 20 minutes. Turn the chicken over and baste with the pan juices. Bake for 15 to 20 minutes longer or until the chicken juices run clear, basting occasionally if necessary.

Yield: 8 servings

Country Cacciatore Chicken

1 green bell pepper, diced
1 red bell pepper, diced
1 yellow bell pepper, diced
1 cup sliced mushrooms
1 small onion, chopped
2 tablespoons minced garlic
$1/2$ cup (1 stick) butter or margarine
1 (13-ounce) bottle Country Bob's All Purpose Sauce
$1/2$ cup packed brown sugar
1 pound boned chicken, cut into bite-sized pieces

Sauté the green, red and yellow peppers, mushrooms, onion and garlic in the butter in a large skillet until lightly browned. Add the Country Bob's All Purpose Sauce and brown sugar and mix well. Place the chicken pieces in a single layer in a 9×13-inch baking pan. Spoon the vegetable mixture over the chicken. Bake, covered, at 350 degrees for 45 minutes. Bake, uncovered, for 15 minutes.

Yield: 4 to 6 servings

Slow-Cooker Chicken and Dumplings

4 boneless skinless chicken breasts
2 tablespoons butter
2 (10-ounce) cans cream of chicken soup
1 onion, finely chopped
1/2 cup Country Bob's All Purpose Sauce
2 (10-count) packages refrigerator biscuits

Place the chicken breasts in a slow cooker. Dot with the butter and add the soup, onion and Country Bob's All Purpose Sauce. Add enough water to cover the chicken. Cover the slow cooker and cook on High for 5 to 6 hours. About 30 minutes before serving time, cut the biscuits into uniform pieces. Add the biscuit pieces to the sauce in the slow cooker gradually, stirring gently to coat with sauce. Cook, covered, for 25 to 30 minutes. Test dumplings for doneness by cutting one in half.

Yield: 4 servings

We Believe
May the Lord direct your hearts into God's love
and Christ's perseverance.
2 Thessalonians 3:5

Slow-Cooker Orange Honey Chicken

6 boneless skinless
chicken breasts
1/2 cup orange juice
1/2 cup chicken broth
1/4 cup honey
1 tablespoon dry mustard
1 tablespoon teriyaki sauce
1/2 cup Country Bob's All Purpose Sauce
1 cup broccoli florets
1 cup cauliflower florets
1 cup sliced carrots
Hot cooked rice

Place the chicken breasts in the slow cooker. Mix the orange juice, broth, honey, dry mustard, teriyaki sauce and Country Bob's All Purpose Sauce in a bowl. Pour over the chicken. Cover and cook on Low for 4 hours. Place the vegetables on top of the chicken; do not stir. Cook, covered, for 1 hour longer. Serve over hot cooked rice.

Yield: 6 servings

Country Bob's Tahiti Chicken

1/4 cup all-purpose flour
3/4 teaspoon Country Bob's Seasoning Salt
1 pound chicken breast tenders
2 tablespoons vegetable oil
1 cup peach preserves
1/4 cup Country Bob's All Purpose Sauce
2 tablespoons soy sauce
1 medium onion, cut into 8 wedges
1 large green bell pepper, cut into strips
1 (16-ounce) can water chestnuts, drained and sliced
Hot cooked rice

Mix the flour and Country Bob's Seasoning Salt in a shallow dish. Roll the chicken tenders in the mixture to coat. Brown the chicken in the oil in a heavy skillet for 2 to 3 minutes on each side; drain. Combine the preserves, Country Bob's All Purpose Sauce, soy sauce and onion in a bowl and mix well. Spoon the mixture over the chicken. Cook, covered, over low heat for 30 minutes, stirring occasionally. Stir in the green pepper and water chestnuts. Cook for 15 minutes longer. Serve over hot cooked rice.

Yield: 4 servings

Creamy Oven-Baked Chicken

8 skinless chicken breasts
1 (4-ounce) can mushroom stems and pieces, drained
1 medium onion, sliced
1 1/2 cups Country Bob's All Purpose Sauce
1 (10-ounce) can cream of mushroom soup
1/2 teaspoon garlic salt

Arrange the chicken breasts bone side up in a baking pan. Layer the mushrooms and onion slices over the chicken. Mix the Country Bob's All Purpose Sauce, soup and garlic salt in a bowl. Spoon over the onions. Bake at 400 degrees for 45 minutes or until the chicken juices run clear.

Yield: 8 servings

We Believe

But you are a chosen people, a royal priesthood, a holy nation, a people belonging to God, that you may declare the praises of him who called you out of darkness into his wonderful light.

1 Peter 2:9

Santa Fe Chicken Stew

2 large green onions, coarsely chopped
2 teaspoons olive oil
2 cups shredded cooked chicken
1 (15-ounce) can kidney beans, drained
1 (8-ounce) can whole kernel corn, drained
1 (14-ounce) can Mexican-style stewed tomatoes
1 (4-ounce) can chopped green chiles
1 (10-ounce) can condensed chicken broth
1/4 cup Country Bob's All Purpose Sauce
2 teaspoons chili powder
1/2 cup chopped fresh cilantro or parsley

Sauté the green onions in the olive oil in a large saucepan for 2 minutes. Stir in the chicken, drained kidney beans, drained corn, undrained tomatoes, undrained green chiles, chicken broth, Country Bob's All Purpose Sauce and chili powder. Simmer, covered, for 10 minutes. Stir in the cilantro.

Yield: 6 to 8 servings

Shrimp Scampi

1 cup (2 sticks) butter
1 cup olive oil
1 teaspoon salt
1 teaspoon pepper
1 teaspoon oregano
1 tablespoon rosemary
2 tablespoons paprika
4 garlic cloves, chopped
3 bay leaves
1/2 cup Country Bob's All Purpose Sauce
3 pounds shrimp, peeled
12 ounces feta cheese, crumbled
1/2 cup bread crumbs

Combine the butter, olive oil, salt, pepper, oregano, rosemary, paprika, garlic, bay leaves and Country Bob's All Purpose Sauce in a saucepan. Heat until the butter melts and the mixture is well blended, stirring frequently. Discard the bay leaves. Layer the shrimp, feta cheese and bread crumbs in a baking dish. Spoon the sauce over the layers. Bake at 375 degrees for 20 minutes.

Yield: 6 to 8 servings

Old Settler's Beans

8 ounces ground beef
8 ounces bacon, crisp-fried and crumbled
1 onion, chopped
$1/2$ cup granulated sugar
$1/2$ cup packed brown sugar
$1/4$ cup Country Bob's All Purpose Sauce
2 tablespoons molasses
$1/2$ teaspoon dry mustard
2 (16-ounce) cans pork and beans
1 (16-ounce) can kidney beans
1 (16-ounce) can butter beans

Cook the ground beef in a large skillet until brown and crumbly; drain. Add the bacon, onion, sugar, brown sugar, Country Bob's All Purpose Sauce, molasses and dry mustard and mix well. Add the undrained beans and mix well. Pour into a greased 9×13-inch baking pan. Bake at 350 degrees for 1 hour.

Yield: 12 to 15 servings

Best-Ever Mushroom and Onion Sauce

1 large onion, sliced
3 tablespoons butter
1 tablespoon sugar
1 (12-ounce) package mushrooms, sliced
3 tablespoons (or more) Country Bob's All Purpose Sauce

Sauté the onion in the butter in a large skillet over medium heat. Sprinkle the sugar over the onion. Cook until the onion is golden. Add the sliced mushrooms. Sprinkle the Country Bob's All Purpose Sauce over the mushrooms and onion. Cook for 4 to 5 minutes, stirring frequently. Serve over grilled steak.

Yield: 4 to 6 servings

We Believe
All Scripture is God-breathed and is useful for teaching, rebuking, correcting and training in righteousness, so that the man of God may be thoroughly equipped for every good work.
2 Timothy 3:16-17

Country Bob's Bacon and Cheese Mashed Potatoes

4 baking potatoes
1 teaspoon salt
$1/2$ cup heavy cream
$1/4$ cup ($1/2$ stick) butter
$3/4$ teaspoon salt
$1/4$ teaspoon pepper
$1/3$ cup Country Bob's All Purpose Sauce
2 cups (8 ounces) shredded sharp Cheddar cheese
$1/4$ cup sour cream
$1/4$ cup chopped fresh chives
8 slices bacon, crisp-fried and crumbled

Cook the potatoes in boiling water to cover with 1 teaspoon salt in a saucepan until fork-tender. Drain the potatoes and return to the saucepan. Add the cream, butter, $3/4$ teaspoon salt and pepper. Place the pan over medium-low heat and mash with a potato masher for 4 to 5 minutes or until the texture is light. Add the Country Bob's All Purpose Sauce, cheese, sour cream, chives and bacon and mix well. Adjust the seasonings.

Yield: 6 to 8 servings

The Ultimate Gravy

1 (15-ounce) can beef, chicken or pork gravy
1¼ cups Country Bob's All Purpose Sauce
1 (15-ounce) can whole berry cranberry sauce
Salt and pepper to taste

Select the gravy flavor that is most compatible with your entrée. Blend the gravy with Country Bob's All Purpose Sauce in a saucepan. Add the cranberry sauce and mix well. Simmer for 5 minutes, stirring frequently. Season to taste.

Yield: 5 cups

We Believe

The Spirit and the bride say, "Come!" And let him who hears say, "Come!" Whoever is thirsty, let him come; and whoever wishes, let him take the free gift of the water of life.

Revelation 22:17

Desserts

We Believe

...that the Church is the body of Christ on earth, empowered by the Holy Spirit, and exists to bring lost people to know Jesus as Savior and Lord.

(Ephesians 4:1-16)

...that Jesus Christ will one day return to earth and reign forever as King of kings and Lord of lords.

(1 Thessalonians 4:13-18)

Butternut Cake

1 cup vegetable shortening
2 cups sugar
4 eggs
2 cups self-rising flour
1 cup milk
1 tablespoon vanilla butternut flavoring
8 ounces cream cheese, softened
$^1/_2$ cup (1 stick) margarine, softened
1 (1-pound) package confectioners' sugar
1 tablespoon vanilla butternut flavoring
1 cup chopped nuts

Cream the shortening and sugar in a mixing bowl until light and fluffy. Add the eggs and beat until well mixed. Add the self-rising flour and milk alternately, beating well after each addition. Beat in 1 tablespoon flavoring. Pour the batter into 3 greased and floured 9-inch cake pans. Bake at 350 degrees until the layers test done. Cool in the pans on wire racks for about 10 minutes. Remove from the pans and cool completely on wire racks. Beat the cream cheese and margarine in a mixing bowl until well blended. Add the confectioners' sugar gradually, beating until of spreading consistency. Beat in 1 tablespoon flavoring. Add the nuts and stir until well mixed. Spread between the layers and over the top and side of the cake.

Yield: 12 to 16 servings

Easy Apple Crunch

3 to 5 apples
1 (3-ounce) package strawberry or
cherry gelatin

1/2 cup (1 stick) margarine
1 cup flour
1 cup sugar

Peel all the apples but 1. Core all the apples; cut into slices. Spread in a 9×13-inch baking pan. Sprinkle with the dry gelatin. Cut the margarine into the flour and sugar in a bowl. Spread over the apples. Bake at 350 degrees for 50 minutes or until the apples are tender.

Yield: 8 to 10 servings

Cherry Delight

3 cups graham cracker crumbs
1/2 cup sugar
1/2 cup (1 stick) butter
16 ounces cream cheese, softened

1 cup confectioners' sugar
1 large carton whipped topping
2 (20-ounce) cans cherry
pie filling

Mix the graham cracker crumbs and sugar in a bowl. Cut in the butter. Press into a 9×13-inch baking pan. Bake at 350 degrees for 10 minutes. Cool. Beat the cream cheese with confectioners' sugar until smooth. Fold in the whipped topping. Spread over the crust. Top with cherry pie filling. Chill thoroughly.

Yield: 8 to 12 servings

Death by Chocolate

1 package brownie mix, prepared
1 (6-ounce) package chocolate
  pudding mix, prepared

2 large cartons whipped topping
2 chocolate-covered toffee bars,
  crushed

Crumble the cooled brownies and set aside. Layer half the brownies, pudding, whipped topping and crushed candy in a large clear trifle bowl or compote. Repeat the layers. Chill until serving time.

Yield: 12 to 16 servings

Earthquake Cake

1 cup coconut
1 cup chopped pecans
1 (2-layer) package German
  chocolate cake mix
8 ounces cream cheese, softened

$1/2$ cup (1 stick) butter, softened
1 teaspoon vanilla extract
1 (1-pound) package
  confectioners' sugar

Sprinkle the coconut and pecans in a greased and floured cake pan. Prepare the cake mix according to the package directions and pour over the coconut and pecans. Blend the cream cheese, butter and vanilla in a bowl. Beat in the confectioners' sugar until smooth. Drop by spoonfuls over the cake batter. Bake at 350 degrees for 35 minutes or until cake tests done. Cool completely.

Yield: 12 to 15 servings

Cream Puff Dessert

1 cup water
1/2 cup (1 stick) margarine
1 cup flour
4 eggs
3 (4-ounce) packages vanilla instant pudding mix
4 cups milk
8 ounces cream cheese, softened
8 ounces whipped topping
Chocolate syrup

Heat the water and margarine to a rolling boil in a saucepan. Remove from the heat. Add the flour all at once and beat vigorously until the mixture forms a ball. Add the eggs 1 at a time and beat until smooth after each addition. Spread in a greased 9×13-inch baking pan. Bake at 400 degrees for 35 to 40 minutes or until golden brown. Cool completely. Combine the pudding mixes with milk in a large bowl. Beat for 2 minutes. Add the cream cheese and beat until smooth and creamy. Spread over the cream puff crust. Cover with whipped topping and drizzle the desired amount of chocolate syrup over the top. Chill for several hours before serving.

Yield: 12 to 15 servings

Fruit Cocktail Cake

2 cups flour
1 1/2 cups sugar
1 tablespoon baking soda
2 eggs
1 tablespoon Country Bob's All Purpose Sauce
1 (16-ounce) can fruit cocktail
1/2 cup (1 stick) butter or margarine
1/2 cup evaporated milk
3/4 cup sugar
1 (6-ounce) can coconut
1/2 to 1 cup chopped nuts

Combine the flour, 1 1/2 cups sugar and baking soda in a mixing bowl and mix well. Add the eggs, Country Bob's All Purpose Sauce and the undrained fruit cocktail. Beat with an electric mixer at medium speed until well mixed. Pour the batter into a greased and floured 9×13-inch cake pan. Bake at 350 degrees for 30 to 35 minutes or until the cake tests done. Combine the butter, evaporated milk and 3/4 cup sugar in a saucepan. Bring to a boil, stirring constantly. Boil for 1 minute, stirring constantly. Add the coconut and nuts and mix well. Spread on the hot cake. Let stand until cool. The flavor is better on the second day.

Yield: 12 to 15 servings

Frozen Fruit Salad

3 cups water
2 1/2 cups sugar
1 (28-ounce) can juice-pack
crushed pineapple
1 (28-ounce) can peaches
1 (10-ounce) jar maraschino
cherries
1 (16-ounce) can pears

6 large bananas, cut up
1 quart strawberries
2 oranges, peeled, sectioned
Seedless grapes
1 (12-ounce) can frozen orange
juice concentrate, thawed
1 orange juice can water

Prepare simple syrup by boiling 3 cups water with 2 1/2 cups sugar until the sugar dissolves completely. Let stand until cool. Prepare canned fruits by draining, reserving the juices and cutting the fruit into bite-sized pieces. Cut the fresh fruit into bite-sized pieces. Combine all the fruit in a large container. Combine the simple syrup, orange juice concentrate, orange juice can water and the reserved fruit juices. Stir into the fruit mixture gently. Place in the freezer and stir several times during the freezing process to distribute the fruit evenly. Serve by letting stand at room temperature until thawed to slushy consistency. Refreeze and thaw as needed. Add or substitute different fruit for variety. Suggestion: Freeze in smaller containers for easier storage and serving. Prepare individual servings by freezing in paper-lined muffin cups.

Yield: variable

Fruit Salsa

1 mango
2 kiwifruit
2 Granny Smith apples
1 quart strawberries
1/4 cup apple jelly
1/2 cup packed brown sugar
Cinnamon Chips

Peel the mango and kiwifruit. Core the apples and stem the strawberries. Cut all the fruit into fine pieces. Combine with the apple jelly and brown sugar in a bowl, mixing well. Chill for 1 hour or longer. Serve with the warm Cinnamon Chips.

Yield: variable

Cinnamon Chips

12 corn or flour tortillas
Butter-flavored nonfat cooking spray
Cinnamon sugar

Spray each tortilla with the cooking spray and sprinkle with cinnamon sugar. Cut each tortilla into 8 wedges and arrange on a baking sheet. Bake at 350 degrees for 5 minutes or until crisp.

Pumpkin Delight

1 (12-ounce) can sweetened
condensed milk
4 eggs
1 1/2 cups sugar
1 (20-ounce) can pumpkin

1 (2-layer) package yellow
cake mix
1 cup (2 sticks) margarine or
butter, melted
1 cup chopped nuts

Mix the first 4 ingredients in a bowl. Pour into a greased 9×13-inch baking pan. Sprinkle the dry cake mix over the top. Drizzle with margarine and sprinkle with the nuts. Bake at 350 degrees for 1 hour or until golden brown.

Yield: 12 to 15 servings

Strawberry Cake Dessert

1 (9×13-inch) yellow cake
1 (6-ounce) package strawberry
gelatin
1 cup boiling water

2 cups strawberry soda
1 (4-ounce) package vanilla instant
pudding mix
1 carton whipped topping

Poke holes all over the hot cake with a fork. Dissolve the gelatin in the boiling water. Stir in the strawberry soda. Pour over the cake. Let stand until cool. Prepare the pudding mix according to the package directions. Blend in the whipped topping. Spread over the cake. Chill for 2 hours to overnight.

Yield: 12 to 15 servings

Strawberry Pizza

1 package refrigerator sugar cookie dough
8 ounces cream cheese, softened
1 cup sour cream
1 cup confectioners' sugar
1 1/4 cups sugar
1/4 cup cornstarch
2 cups cold water
1 (3-ounce) package strawberry gelatin
1 quart fresh strawberries, cut into halves

Cut the cookie dough into slices and arrange in a pizza pan with slices touching. Press the slices together to form an even crust. Bake according to the package directions until golden brown. Cool completely. Combine the cream cheese, sour cream and confectioners' sugar in a bowl and beat until creamy. Spread over the cookie crust. Mix the sugar and cornstarch in a saucepan. Stir in the water. Bring to a boil, stirring constantly, and cook until clear. Stir in the gelatin until completely dissolved. Cool completely. Arrange the strawberries cut side down on the cream cheese mixture. Spoon the glaze over the strawberries. Chill in the refrigerator. Garnish with whipped cream.

Yield: 8 to 12 servings

Toffee Bread Pudding

2 (8-ounce) packages prepared cinnamon
rolls (without icing)
2 eggs
1/4 cup packed brown sugar
2 cups milk
1 teaspoon vanilla extract
1/2 cup almond toffee bits
Caramel ice cream topping
Whipped cream

Cut the cinnamon rolls into quarters and let stand, uncovered, overnight to dry out. Place the roll pieces in an 8-inch square baking dish that has been lightly sprayed with nonstick cooking spray. Whisk the eggs with the brown sugar in a medium bowl. Whisk in the milk and vanilla. Pour over the rolls and sprinkle the toffee bits over the top. Let stand for 15 minutes. Bake at 350 degrees for 45 to 50 minutes or until a knife inserted in the center comes out clean. Serve warm with caramel topping drizzled over each serving. Garnish with a dollop of whipped cream.

Yield: 6 to 8 servings

Incredible Fudge

12 ounces Velveeta cheese
1 cup (2 sticks) butter or margarine
6 (1-ounce) squares unsweetened baking chocolate
2 tablespoons Country Bob's All Purpose Original Sauce
2 (1-pound) packages confectioners' sugar
1 teaspoon vanilla extract
1 1/2 cups chopped pecans (optional)

Place the Velveeta, butter, chocolate and Country Bob's All Purpose Original Sauce in a large microwave-safe bowl. Microwave on High for 2 to 4 minutes, stirring every minute until the mixture is smooth and well blended. Place the confectioners' sugar in a large mixing bowl. Add the chocolate mixture gradually, beating with an electric mixer at medium speed until well blended after each addition. Beat in the vanilla. Stir in the pecans. Pour the fudge into a greased 9×13-inch pan. Smooth the top. Cover and refrigerate for several hours or until firm. Cut into squares. Store in the refrigerator.

Yield: 4 pounds

Index

To order additional copies of
The Original Country Bob's Cookbook *and to*
order our products, please call 1-800-373-2140,
or visit our website at www.countrybobs.com.